The Philosophy of Unclean Things

poems by

Rosemarie Dombrowski

Finishing Line Press
Georgetown, Kentucky

The Philosophy of
Unclean Things

ACKNOWLEDGMENTS

"Seven Days" appeared in *The Hartskill Review*, August 2014.
"Civil War" & "The Resurrection of Lazarus with Worms" appeared in *The Poet's
Billow* (Pangea Prize Finalists), summer 2015.
"That Time we Watched the Sunset on a Swing" appeared in *He Said to Me:
Conversations That Inspired us to Write*, the blog of Five Oaks Press and Foiled
Crown Books, September 2015.
"Bagua and the Art of Loss" appeared in *Spilled Milk*, November 2015.
"Infidelity" appeared in *Stonecoast Review*, December 2015.
"An Inexact Taphonomy" appeared in In Sight: *An Ekphrastic Collaboration
between Eye Lounge and Four Chambers Press*, March 2016.
"for cummings and the very beautifully suddenly rendering death and forever,"
The Wax Paper, March 2016.
"The Psychology of Expatriation I, II, & III" are forthcoming in *Anthro/Poetics:
An Anthology on Culture and Writing about Culture*.

Publisher: Leah Maines

Editor: Christen Kincaid

Cover Art: Tawny Kerr

Author Photo: Mark Sunman

Cover Design: Elizabeth Maines

Printed in the USA on acid-free paper.
Order online: www.finishinglinepress.com
        also available on amazon.com

Author inquiries and mail orders:
Finishing Line Press
P. O. Box 1626
Georgetown, Kentucky 40324
U. S. A.

Table of Contents

*For the obsessive-compulsive, the germaphobic,
the ornithophobic, the superstitious, the numerological,
the self-flagellating, the fatalistic environmentalists,
and the part-time expatriates.*

I. Unclean Things

Civil War

The dead bird is a kind of song.

I think about the end of Lorca, the act of loyalty,
the incidental things.

And I wonder what we've really discovered,
what anyone truly knows before their exile.

Maybe just this: that both sides of a double-sided coin
can be wrong.
That anything moral is a dilemma.

According to Spanish legend, the king of crickets
steals the voices of boys,
leaving them mute.

According to you, this is why you're here:
for the truce-making.
And for the words.

Exile

The decapitated bird is like the king of Spain,
and since we discovered it,
we've referred to the East wall
as the site of exile.

I question you about the promenades
and the backyard muck.
Why the promenades?
Why the backyard muck?

You blame the dysentery.
I say the death of the citrus was infectious.

People say that you're young and it won't last,
but I keep thinking of diseases and the dead bird,
how permanent it all seems.

Dead Birds

In Germany, a girl is possessed by demons,
stops eating, bites off the head of a dead bird.

In China, duck thieves are forced to carry
the stolen birds in their mouths as punishment.

According to the people of New Guinea,
dead birds are the ornaments of war:
a bloody spearhead, a beaded belt,
a necklace made from the bones of a heron.

In Gardner's film, the adage of the Dani tribe is
people, like birds, must die.

After viewing it, Lowell said he seemed to
stagger inside [him]self,
that it had a *guilty significance,*

the terrible thing [being] that they
remind us so much of ourselves.

The Philosophy of Unclean Things

Swine

The village of La Gloria was quick
to blame the pigs.
They knew they were cursed and unclean.

When his body began to ache,
they called him boy zero—
niño cero, the boy with the plague.

Four days later, he made a miraculous recovery.

Bovine

The Petrograd Conservatory was the first
to see his feet,
though no one recalls the shape of his toes.

In Europe, there was Tamara and Alexandra,
Sergei of the *Ballets Russes*
and the death of his knee.

America was where he lost his equilibrium.
No one knew that the mad cow
had been destroying his brain for a decade.

Without balance, the body is like water,
squeezed from a sponge.

Infidelity

I. Bird

You come home on a Monday and I tell you
that I'm in love with the decomposing bird
that's been tucked under the hibiscus for months.
I make you look at its sad little sack of bones,
the fuzz trapped inside the marrow
that's melting into the soil.

I tell you that it had a four-chambered heart
and practiced the art of call-and-response.
I tell you that social monogamy should be
declared a religion.
I'm convinced that my obsession with tea
has to do with the fossils of birds found in China.

You tell me that you collected porcelain birds
when you were ten.
I tell you that this one isn't my first.

II. Prairie Dog

When we discover the prairie dog,
I make you photograph its decapitated body,
file the images under
things that need to be identified or explained.

But I want you to know that I'm not always like this,
that I have faith in things that aren't finite—
like pick-up games of marbles on the playground,
cats with rubber balls and the persistence of weeds.

I want to be able to tell you
that I've scooped up the carcass,
tossed it into the foul, green bin
with the turkey gizzards and the egg shells,
the beer bottles that the neighbors are too lazy to recycle.

I want to believe that everything rots for a reason,
that the periodic table of elements
is a book of vegetarian recipes in various states of decay,
that electrons will always be harmonious with protons,
that once things align, they never veer off course.

But we both know better.

The Missouri Bluebird Study

Someone once told me that blue eyes aren't really blue,
that everything is an optical illusion
named after the physicist Lord Rayleigh.

But then I saw you and your wide-eyed,
seven-blue-inches of innocence
on an early spring night.
And I remembered my grandmother telling me
that it was perfectly agreeable to fall in love
with anything that perches
on the branches of a flowering dogwood
because they have exceptional resistance
to disease.

And though an ornithologist once said
that everything depends upon the species,
the blue on your back never changes—
like the ghastly blue of the sky before a tornado,
or the blue of the blue hour, which only reveals
the inferiority of the red
as it passes straight into space,
scattering the blue back down to earth.

And for those forty minutes, the world is
a staggering blue infinity—
like the bluebirds of Missouri, mid-March or later,
or the cobalt of Chinese porcelain from the 9th Century,
or the ultramarine of Mary's robes
in the painting entitled *Virgin of Humility*, circa 1430.

A Bird Is the Heart of Memory

Only the birds can disregard
borders, make them invisible
like the shifts between time zones
or the drops in the ocean floor.

If Li Po could hear this,
I'd tell him to build it in the shape of a birdhouse.
I'd warn him that even a poet can misread
the sounds of birds,
the sack of a human heart.

If my mother could hear this,
I'd recite the nursery rhyme about Blackbirds
from memory:
Fly away Jack. Fly away Jill.

In the Southwest, the sparrow prefers to skulk
in the thickets, and the roadrunner is a shaman—
its feathers protecting babies,
its X-shaped footprints confusing evil spirits.

In the Midwest, the bluebirds would wail for hours.
In the spring, they'd dream
of dying in the forest.
By late July, the yard would be filled with
impossible pieces of puzzle.

The Resurrection of Lazarus with Worms

I'm circling the yard like an odyssey,
like a mythological tale
about a boy who adored turpentine and oils,
who was obsessed with the lives of 16th Century Venetians.

And like any lover of frescos,
he was plagued by an *insatiable perfectionism*,
and so he recited incantations for the dead,
and he told me that the resurrected can't make love,
and that angels were just another word for ecstasy.

So when I found the bird lodged in the river rock,
its one wing still nervously fluttering,
I thought of Titian, and how he would hide his paintings for years,
as though the art of capturing something
in the act of dying was always too imperfect.
And I thought of Lazarus, and what it means to have
nine times to die, and how worms must feel
when they crawl along the bodies of the dead,
or slither down the throats of birds.

And I remembered the ecstatic tone of Dante
as he instructed Calliope *to strike a higher key,
to raise poetry from the dead.*

And so I crouched over the fragile body,
and I began whispering a prayer that could
resuscitate the dying,
hoping not to revive the pigeons in the alley.

The Figure a Bird Makes

He said that the job of art was to clean it,
like a potato that's been brushed.

I think about Frost cleaning the American vegetables,
razing a path through its cities,
boring holes in the dirt for the seeds of love-sickness
to be gingerly dropped and tended.

Strip it to form, find its fulfillment.

I retrieve the antique chair from the garage,
paint it robin's-egg-blue and imagine
a bird perched on its tray
in the middle of the yard in August.
I scratch a pattern of scuffling claws
across its arms and legs.

When I walk along the canal,
I might see the remains of something,
photograph the rotting body,
prop the image against the chalky blue slats
already parched from the sun.

This is how words become deeds.

Taxidermy

after Annette Messager's Les Repos des Pensionnaires

Spread their legs like delicate twigs.
Splay their wings like umbrellas.
Resist the urge to split the limbs like a wish,
to pass half to your uncle who's finishing up
his goulash to your right.

Determine the size of the crocheting needle
used to knit miniature yellow sweaters
and striped scarves.
Make tiny ankle tags for the curator
of North American ornithology.

Visit the taxidermist on Roosevelt Street.
Before leaving, ask her
what their bodies might smell like next summer.

Believe her when she tells you
that a sparrow is a spice in the night,
dust-bathing in agave-arsenic soil,
preening and singing in the dead colonies of Phoenix
or some well-ventilated garage.

An Inexact Taphonomy
After Tawny Kerr's A System of Strings, mixed media installations

The body of grandmother inside the stomach of a bird

Slice open the gizzard like an unripe olive,
small and insignificant,
indicating that the bird died
during the summer.
Inside it, a jump-ring, some strands of
long, gray hair, a button tangled in
burnt-orange yarn, shards of
a femur, a tumorous colon.

Unlike bone, fruit and insects
are easily absorbed.

Once infected, the fungus rots
the throat of the swallow, rendering it
silent and depressed.

The body of an insect inside the root of a citrus tree

The roots are limbs
giving birth to fibers,
tangled like feeding tubes.
Excavate the root ball
with all ten fingers.
Inside it, uncover a miniature skeleton,
a pair of fragile wings radiating
in every direction.

The fungi follow the spring flush.
Once infected, a tree may begin
to swallow excessively,
its fibers clogging like straws.

The skin of a woman inside the stamen of a flower

Begin skinning the leg, removing
the follicles and capillaries
until the epidermal shavings are coiling
around themselves. Make symmetrical towers
and admire the way they flower
from the center of emptiness
like an artichoke or *agave chihuahuana.*

Stitch them together with cellulose.
Paint them a faded cerulean.
Bake them on stones that will
litter the desert floor.

An egg inside the belly of an anemone

Trapped in the sac of a belly,
the daisies drown
in the *bellis perennis* of language,
in corpses of Latin
suspended from twine.

Bleach the skeletons of reefs
until they morph into paper.
Flatten the sheets
with a stalk of bamboo—
the layers clinging like cocoons,
suffocating with indigenous creatures.

A staple inside the intestines of jicama

The body outgrows the membrane.
The staples are inserted
at odd angles
to stop the bleeding of
agua and nutrients.
The tips are painted white
for penance,
for suffering,
for things the body recognizes
as decay.

Wrap the fibers tightly
like dressing cloth.
Attach a bird's wing,
broken from the fall.
Poison the remaining insects
with its seed,
adding cilantro and lemon,
ginger to taste.

A rose strangled by intangible fire

There's madness inside the flame—
bundles of colorless thorns
rimmed with magenta.

The root-stem is a drawer
where things are stored for the winter,
coated with the mucous of life, pressed
between layers of memory and sulfurous reds.

When you bind the heart with string,
the threads begin to fray, depositing tiny fibers
into clogged passages,
rotting like the constant stench of impermanence.

A bag of starlings inside the legs of a dancer

The birds have become a nuisance,
like your pin-tips and string-scars.
The noose made of sinew tightens
around the circumference of your thigh
like a dance of dying muscles.

The abdominal cavity is a choreographer,
sustaining itself on bacteria
and frenetic spinning
until there's nothing to maintain,
no faith except in
the botany of seedlings.

II. Obsessions

What I Know about Desire

I want to avoid naming names
or discussing the actual history of things.
I want to retrace the routes of would-be explorers.

I want to feel the crush of bodies
and the weight of unread papers,
the steam of a coffeehouse or a pot on the stove.

I know what it means to be compulsive.
I know that the violation of one code
is generally forgivable by most.

I know what it means when you say that
the stagecoach is a runaway train,
that nothing historical is worth burning
unless it's riddled with disease.

You say that survival is tentative.
I say that survival is hard.
Survival, like desire, is always about the etceteras.

The Beginning of Euphoria

The floor was newly tiled and they were dancing
to the Flaming Lips.

By the second track, she'd caught a moth
with a spoon and watched a spider
fall prey to the raspberry jelly.
By the time they got to the B sides,
he asked her if she'd let the world explode
in exchange for a Nobel Prize in physics.

The floor was cold that day despite the weather,
and God was queer and possibly made of plastic,
and everyone was praised for their oddities
because that's what the satellites
that orbit the heart truly desire.

By the time the album ended,
they had well-surpassed the century-mark,
but it felt like they were just beginning.

Euphoria

By early summer, he was strumming chords
in the middle of a field,
burning incense and swilling Old Style
while wearing a fedora and a pair of plaid shorts.
His frame was thin, like the shallow chest of a boy,
like the fragility of apple-coring,
like the removal of anything
from the center of anything
without disturbing the exterior beyond recognition.

For weeks, this was how they lived—
the act of transforming noise into measures,
measures into music, music into operatic sagas
on a screen where liquids were being pushed
through the chambers of the heart
and the beats were luminescing in a one-two pattern
like half notes in a four-four time signature,
the melody repeating itself until
it reaches the coda and he asks her
if she likes the composition.

Why Gregory Should Leave Sarah
For GS

On Prairie Hill with Sarah,
everything's back-lit, front-lit, sun-lit, moon-lit,
perfectly staged and buttressed with baskets of flowers,
abstract covers of obscure books,
pages stained with the corpses of flowers
extracted from even obscurer books.

Love will make you do that, and this:
cover one eye with tousled curls,
write something about a silent film
then take a photograph of what you've written.

But Gregory has always been sad—
sad since Emily and the retaining wall,
sad underneath all those stylish hats,
sad despite the back-lighting, the front-lighting,
the natural-lighting,
sad despite Sarah's teased hair
and the stench of wildflowers,
sad about the talking around him and over him
and through him,
the incessant talking that left him deducing
that skin is just skin
no matter what you might think
in the beginning.

Gregory Is a Metaphor
For GS

He tried to board flight 422 from Minneapolis
to Jackson, but the agent's gloves were unclean
from all the rifling and the leaking of liquids,
the suspicions of unidentified garments.

He missed two flights,
made a few calls to Sarah,
tried pulling himself together
by writing a poem—something about love
and how it makes you want to stuff paper in a hole,
bright red paper with sex all over it,
and you keep stuffing and stuffing
until everything becomes a lie
and the lies eventually become the truest parts.

Like how you know when something isn't good for you—
like the feeling of misguided love or a chemical addiction,
a sickening obsession that increases
with each irrational reaction to public surfaces
or the sound of someone clearing his throat.

And you know that these justifications
via his justifications
are insanity personified—
like the insanity the settles in
when someone doesn't know your name
and isn't watching,
but you can't stop acting like they are.

A Dear John Letter to Gregory
For GS

Freedom is just a metaphor for another kind of captivity.

There's a book between the covers that
recounts the history of addiction,
how you were released from the institution
and not a day too soon.

That's what love will do to you—
coil your intestines into un-wrench-able knots.
Make you love-junk sick until there's nothing left
but a phrase of music, the hands on a clock.

I want the book that you're writing
to open with an epigraph from the *Inferno*—
I answer without fear of being shamed.
I want it to be a story about someone who's resistant
to germs and the fear of amputation.
I want the eighth chapter to recount the details
of someone who's lived through the pre-insanity years
and the post-insanity archives while recording
the genealogy of hypochondria.

I don't want to be curious about the important things anymore.

An Open Letter to Gregory

There's nothing left but distance
and the stench of patchwork sheets,
the negative color of your skin
against a saturated plane of navy.

The feminists say that you want us
to save ourselves from sanity,
ingest poisonous flowers,
maybe stop eating altogether.

I trace the crease of your khakis,
the image of your hand disappearing
into your pocket and the blankness
of your swarthy eyes.
I'd be a monster if I asked you to grow me a child.

Maybe you're hiding behind winter now,
a wooly corner of a bungalow
next to a shelf of books—
an image of a covered wagon, a rabbit
in a pea-green sea.
Maybe you're feeling yourself without touching.
Maybe you've been doing it for the last two years.

I've traced you to a county in Mississippi
with a population of 19,000, the place
where all the members of the Bundren family
went to die or go mad,
where the river still whispers
that you *knew without the words.*

Francesca Woodman in Black and White

black

Your body is dusty, dappled with resins and glue,
your skin like a robe made from
the dirty skin of women.

Sometimes you crouch beneath windows,
hiding yourself from the light—
crotch to wire, snake to bird, hair like vines
crawling along brick,
winding back to the crotch like a map of Florence.

Sometimes you dangle from strings,
between walls with crumbling plaster.
Sometimes you contain boys
because you love them sometimes—
the way they erect themselves
without spines, the bedraggled hair
and the stares of Roman lusting.

The concrete is ancient and cold
through the haze of your lens.

You reach for the only flesh you can see,
and you touch it, and you fall.

white

You duck behind light,
crucify yourself in doorways,
wrap yourself in wallpaper wings.

You write notes in gibberish
along the small of your back,
phrases you never need to translate

because they go directly to your hands—
hands that are pressed against glass,
legs wrapped in twine that spirals like serpents,
their forked tongues inching toward your pubis,
your hair snaggled into a Gordian knot.

You slump into the corner rocker,
eat the husks of animals with a rusty fork,
stab at your nipples like olives.

You wear a polka dotted dress.
You gag yourself with curtain ties.
You never tell him not to write this.

III. Superstitions

for cummings and the very beautifully suddenly rendering death and forever

Take what's left and place an ampersand between it.
Finish the rest when you're on a trail
in the forest, wandering
through your head like a clearing filled with
jay-blues and thrushes, and when there's snow
on the trail you know that you're an existentialist
on the page of a Wallace Stevens poem,
except it's too cold to watch
the blackbirds and their variations
of bird-meter and wing-rhyme,
so you've brought lenses and a notebook
for sketching the things you're hearing
into a new existence, something that will flash
before your eyes days later,
when *your head is a living forest full of songbirds.*

for DiPrima and the school of breathing magic in the borealis party

No problem, she says, because it's not the party that's the problem but something at the edge of history that has to do with numbers and cosmology and the work that no one's doing outside the coming-and-going of their window-living and ballroom-wandering, which has nothing to do with *starvation* except the *imagination* and the *war against* it; so when we arrive at the party and everyone's talking politico and the Texas border and there's nothing even remotely vegan on the buffet, I'll lean over and whisper the firmament of god's toe into your ear, and the sound will vibrate through the *intellectus* canal until it reaches your frightened heart, where the nothingness makes a barking sensation that rattles our coffee mugs and our tiny muffin plates and can only be a sign of the fierceness that folksingers have gifted us, the kind that a claustrophobic thought could explode from, like the priestess seeing with the *eyes of gods* [and] *insects* while waving a book of revolution and an array of healing herbs.

That Time I Read Melville to a Coltrane Soundtrack

I open my mouth like a whale.
Someone's playing Coltrane in the back of my throat.
The table is painted a rare shade of aquamarine.
The room is a brisk sixty-three degrees.

I have a theory that's nothing like a theory:
retrieve the harpoon and leave my thoughts
to bounce off constellations,
make cirrus waves of sound.

The boys are playing their hearts out,
which reminds me of the boy who
stole my book from the choir loft,
the flagpole beside the abandoned schoolhouse
in the foreground,
the junkyard filled with carburetors
and other useless things behind

Bagua and the Art of Loss

She makes him kiss her before she *feng shuis* the birds (cardinal above blue jay), alphabetizes the books she almost read last month. He watches as she sweeps the crumbs one-by-one into the dustpan. She tells him that a woman is a fork and a man is a spoon.

They sit on bright green Adirondacks facing southward, eat pink ladies until their toes are sweet and they can sense the monsoon rains rounding the western corner. He wishes he could change the song that's playing in his head, the one about the girl who hitchhikes north to Santa Fe and reminds him of his dead sister.

But he can't, because his mind is like a View-Master, and he's clicking between the aerial map and the nearby motel, the creek bed and the muddied tank top, the glasses that were never found. She tells him when there's that much pain in the world, we're forced to make little piles of order wherever we can; so she takes his hand, and they crouch down to the bottom shelf, and he watches as she runs her finger over the spines: Whitman, W., Williams, W., Wright, J., Yeats, W.B.

Numerology

She started crying around 11:45.
She wiped her eyes several times without counting.
There were 14 minutes remaining in the episode.
She wrote something between 12:05 and 12:15
that she would never give him.
It was the 19th of July.
She was 29.
Or maybe 19.

She was surely the sum-total
of Midwestern values gone wrong,
bravado channeled from her old-world roots,
his tuft of bleached hair
multiplied by his love of linguistic fucking,
his loathing of pickles
divided by the two sets of initials
they carved into the table
beneath the library's entrance,
the ones they'd drawn in the dust
with their fingertips a few weeks before.
More times than she could count.

Superstitions: Theirs

They threw a coin into the fountain,
made a wish on a streamer of light
as he turned the key clockwise three times.

They were seated at a table
when the bell chimed nine.
They toasted to stability and persisted
in their drinking,

tossing pinches of salt over their shoulders,
like children scattering the ashes
of a relative they barely knew
and would never see again.

Superstitions: Hers

He picked up a penny.
She found a pin.
They placed both inside the red leather purse
that she carried for protection

as they huddled under the stars,
shared a quince like ancient Roman lovers
listening to owls they didn't know the species of.

She wondered if dropping a sock
was akin to dropping a glove,
which led her to wonder
how long she should wait for a stranger
to assist her in picking up either.

She wondered if carrying a hacksaw
through the house
was as bad as carrying an axe,
if fingers that were both long and crooked
foretold both wealth and impulsivity.

She wondered if it was safe
to light only three candles
if one of them had three wicks.
And speaking of fires,
she wondered if she could even purchase
a pair of bellows.

She determined that the rules
of eclipses and bees and cauls
were too convoluted to commit to memory.
She wondered whether or not birds were drawn to
a cappella versions of Latin hymns.

She had done literally everything forbidden
with an umbrella,
which prompted her to tell him
that even pigeons were superstitious,
that the three-peck study of experimental behavior
had proven it.

That's right, she said,
proven it.

The Final Frame Is Wonderment

a girl back-lit behind a row of bars; the location of the history of revelation.

The boy's foot is on the fender,
and they're passing a single lighter
between their fingers,
smoking a cheap pack of Parliaments
that's been dented by the stitches of his pocket,
the way it molded to his body
when he sat to eat or drive.

(Everything touches everything.
Inanimate objects are learning
what it means to make contact.)

a letter containing phrases that haven't been accessed for decades.

In it, she discovers absurdist theories
and conceptual verse,
jargon pierced through its center
with a small knife and meticulous diction.

It's part manifesto, part beautiful lie.

(...the symbolic value
of a deer in the moonlight,
the unbearable revelations
behind Adagio for Strings.)

the photos that never existed are arranged in an album that doesn't
contain pages.

His tooth is chipped, badly,
and his lip is swollen from the asphalt.
He's holding a glass of whiskey,
eating a slice of apple
that she peeled in the sink.

The grass is twining between his toes.
A stray cat crawls into his lap.
He's holding a book by Kathryn Starbuck
(*Griefmania*)
before he disappears from the page.

(The final frame is blank,
but like the pages, it's never really empty.)

The Time We Watched the Sunset on a Swing

You remind me of curry.
You buy more bananas than anyone could eat in a week.
You talk about the florists of New York,
the speak-easys that sell poems and absinthe behind curtains.
I tell you that art and debauchery
should always be paired with a heavier wine.
You tell me we should bike to the nearest café,
make some barometric waves,
craft something that resembles a wild animal
out of the hides of an endangered species.

I find you in the sauce aisle on a Tuesday.
We talk about cheeses that are better when grated.
You reach out to touch me because you want to know
the horizon of my torso.
It's sort of like the sunset—the waiting,
the anticipating, the wanting to know
where one thing ends and the next begins.

I wonder if you remember the time
that we watched the sunset on a swing.
And the sand was working its way between my toes.
And the light was dipping behind the mountain.

IV. Unnatural Disasters

Seven Days

1.
I am not the Eve to your Adam,
and though I've read the story a hundred times,
I'm still not sure what a white apple tastes like.

2.
The first glass smelled like whiskey,
and so did the second.
I watched as you slid them across the counter,
pondering what it means to be weak of heart.

3.
Everyone was stuffed with bread and wine,
so you took us on a scavenger hunt
in the night sky: first, Orion's femur,
then, the ulna of the dogs.

You reminded us that you can't have the Blue Period
without the basics, that no one
would love the centos if it weren't for
their love of the originals.

4.
We climbed up to the rock
where things are discovered,
where the archives
can be arranged into hundreds of stories.
We wove them together and created a legend.

5.
It all seemed so Greek—the bull and the swan and
the flying too close to the sun.

The plot lingered like winter.

6.
We obsessed over etymology the way
some people obsess over intimacy.
On the sixth night, we used the word
saturation in a sentence.

We knew we had reached
the point at which something
has absorbed as much liquid, solid, or gas
as is physically possible.

7.
We wondered why certain games
were based purely on chance.
Still, we knew there were rules
that could never be broken.

Catalina Recovery Project

Everything was drizzling,
and there was wine on our knuckles,
and you were humming The Stones
while I obsessed over drowning,
began cataloging the things
that could survive without oxygen or blood—
the tiny jellyfish in the Mediterranean,
the *cimex lectularius* in cooler climes.

We drank through the afternoon.
We drank for the island,
for the mausoleum of secrets
and the ones who didn't survive.

We took a dozen self-portraits
on the cliff, a handful on the docks.
We didn't write our names in the captions.
We didn't connect ourselves with ampersands.

Slowly It Enters

Like a tractor into the grass,
its wheels sinking.

Like light passing through atoms
its photons absorbed.

Like the Karnatake Express
rolling into New Delhi.

But mostly like intruders entering King Tut's tomb—
slowly, desperately as they watched,
the debris removed from the passage
until they finally made a breach,
until the door stood clear before them
and Dr. Carter shouted back to Lord Carnarvon,
yes, wonderful things, yes, wonderful things.

Times Beach

The guinea pigs are dead,
and the horses are collapsing in nearby stables.
The Meramec River is flooding the town,
and no one knows how much Agent Orange
is seeping into bathtubs.

Everyone evacuates but the elderly couple,
wrapped in a homemade afghan,
watching the Lawrence Welk dancers
waltz across the screen.

We drive along Route 66 until we see
the mounds of debris.
The agency assures us that there are
"no significant health risks for visitors."

We think about disasters, priorities,
the lies that men tell.
We watch an unsuspecting family buying soda
from one of the many vending machines
in the park.

Saturday Night

He wants to bed the middle-aged woman
at the blue-collar bar.

He wants to bed a host of women,
get his share, do his living.

She waits in a parking lot across town
with an alcoholic lawyer, yet to be disbarred.

She worries that the filth of the night
will stick to her sole.

She worries that someone has stunted
the evolution of the universe, diminished God's grace.

She worries that the moment has been compromised,
and that the only infinite moment is now.

Anatomy of a Relationship

obsession

She's sick with longing
for the word-gardener, the pipe-fixer,
the throat-bleeding cannibal.

His name lodges between
the lip blister and the frontal lobe.

She understands nothing,
takes up smoking,
follows him around the country
on someone else's dime,
is frequently mistaken for someone tragic.

Whatever he gives will be enough
and not enough,
more than most.

But letting go means catastrophe.

guilt

At fifty, he has yet to marry.
When he asks, she declines the offer.

But guilt is good, and they both know it,
like the eyes of Christ know,
like how you know when you see a freak-show,
how it battles deep in your soul.

So he tells her she's a strange act of God,
the water that drowns a man in Costa Rica.

And he concludes that love is not a flavor,
that love is kinetic—
like the act of shoveling rock,
like the plot of a good story.

fatalism

She scans the pages for evidence of
the lover or the wild dog.
Already three marriages
and too much wine.

This is not the story of the woman
she thought it was.
He has cut out his tongue
for the sake of silence.

Still, no one is happy.

For the Death of Things

1.
I tell you to wash your feet,
to stop cleaning your brushes
in unventilated rooms.

You tell me that you saw Georgia O'Keefe
suspended from a string,
holding a tea set
that no one knew the origins of.

2.
You were running laps inside a drugstore.
You bought Tequila and gum
while I perched myself on the counter
like a skittish bird.

You always had a novel by Anaya in your backpack.
After the baby, you strung the last few beads
onto the rosary.

3.
We both knew what lilies meant—
futility, like an unopened bottle of whiskey
or the sweaty handkerchief on the seat.

When it rained that night,
it flooded your complex like an omen.
As if to taunt me, the flowers lived for days.

V. Displacements

After the Incident I

The cold steel cracks into
the back of your aging skull,
the dented panel of your car.
I want to split you apart like lentils
soaking in a bath of broth.

Outside, the birds are bathing
in a concrete bowl.
The pedestal is cracked,
like your head and the steel frame.
Like the lentils.

The next morning, one of the birds
is floating face-down.
I wrap it in a rag from the garage.
I'm thinking about the city
in Cheyenne County, Kansas
where less than 447 people remain.

The cloth that you wrap me in
is flimsy and smells like gardenias.
(That's what my mother would notice.)

After the Incident II
After Parra's Weirded Out Mural Installation

The swans are eating swans,
and someone has pierced himself
twice with swords.

A man carries the carcass of a swan
without moving, which is how most men move
when the Phoenix is rising,
when it's fast-burning the skin
of a fawn toward his heels.

The can-can girl is eating her swollen toe,
and the canon-shooting woman
has tossed her head like a trapeze flier dropped,
like a fat lady doing acro-yoga in pumps.

Everyone is naked *most of the time,*
which makes it like a circus
without actually being one,
a projection in permeant ink
on a temporary panel of wall
inside concentric discs of areolas,
between the legs of the man on the scaffolding
who seems to be collecting ink-feathers
and nipple shrapnel
in the teeth of his phone,
the horns of a bull in a star-spangled helmet.

Dislocation

The scene repeats itself in slow motion:
the plane loses altitude,
hovers at ten-thousand feet.

You wade in the river.
Orion pours from the spout.
The fish continue to swim frenetically.

The women in Kente are rocking you
against their breasts,
suctioning sand from your nostrils.

Traces of light slip in through the crags
as they carry you to higher ground.

You call someone who isn't your father,
briefly discuss the possibility of tremors.

It's hardly a conversation, but he's still convinced
that direction can be found on maps.

The Psychology of Expatriation I

You hitchhike at dusk,
make your way toward an unmarked gulch,
an easel teetering in gravel.
Inside, a man is smudging charcoal onto canvas
in the shape of the madness
between your legs.

In the bathroom, you ask yourself
where the voices have gone.
You can't recall the name
of the medication they give to soldiers
in malaria-heavy countries,
the source of homeland psychosis.

You wait until the water runs clear
then brush your teeth under the tap:
no visible parasites, no bloody retching.
The test for embryonic fluid is negative.

Tomorrow, the room will be empty,
the unusable plywood soaking up water in the delta.

Something is missing besides the voices,
but you don't know where to find it.

The Psychology of Expatriation II

Somewhere near the prime meridian,
the yellow warbler sings about sweetness.
Someone else is speaking Ewe mixed with Twi.

By afternoon, the cars are colliding
on unnamed roads,
the pigeon-words rapidly firing
holes into the dent above the wheel.
The blood of the goat is a brothy shade of red.

We sit silently in the back seat,
wondering when we'll see
this side of the Atlantic again.

The Psychology of Expatriation III

The boat is rocking, and castor oil coats
the lining of our stomachs.
The sea and everyone who drank from the bottle
is sick. Even the air smells schizophrenic,
the moon in reverse on the puddle of water.

We measure our worth in *cidis*,
so we spend the afternoon translating
words into units: the slave ships looping
the screen, the Atlantic maddening
under crests of memory.

A few streets away from the seamstress,
a man in a booth sells bootleg wine.
Everything worth finding requires the crossing
of borders or state lines: sparklers,
palm wine, endangered animal hides.

In this hemisphere, the sky sings
lullabies to the villages,
and the cocoas fall like percussion.

Omissions

I make up stories about gazelles,
color-code the Capes and the castles,
fabricate the gaps between here and Kumasi.

I lie about sleeping with men
who covered themselves in coal,
about the dead goats and the August psychosis,
the rice paddies and the villagers eating squirrels.

I'll never tell you about the market,
or the words I shouted in Twi,
or the ring made of brass
that he slipped on my pinky in the cab.

Postscript

I want to make you a bracelet out of
stone beads, uneven strands
that I've been wearing for two-hundred years.

I want to tell you that there are more languages
in the Niger-Congo family
than there are years between us.

I want to chart the rhythms
of some ancient, tribal music,
gossip and catalogue the dead.

I want to tell you about the oceans
that didn't swallow you,
how I ate avocado for days;

the way I duct-taped your drum to my body,
the sound coursing
through my veins like cables.

Rosemarie Dombrowski is the founder of rinky dink press, the co-founder and host of the Phoenix Poetry Series, and an editor for *Four Chambers*. She has received four Pushcart nominations, was a finalist for the Pangea Poetry Prize in 2015, and was nominated for the Best of the Net Anthology in 2016 (Sundress publications). Her first collection, *The Book of Emergencies* (Five Oaks Press, 2014), was the recipient of the 2016 Human Relations Indie Book Award for Poetry (personal challenge category). She's a Senior Lecturer at Arizona State University's Downtown campus where she teaches courses on radical poetics, women's literature, and creative ethnography. Additionally, she was selected in December 2016 to be the inaugural poet laureate of Phoenix, AZ.

www.ingramcontent.com/pod-product-compliance
Lightning Source LLC
Chambersburg PA
CBHW021202090426
42740CB00008B/1203